Leadership

High-performing Team, Retaining Top-notch Talent, And
Developing Future Leaders With Self-assurance

(Highly Effective Characteristics Of Effective Leaders)

Alois-Uwe Klemm

TABLE OF CONTENT

Introduction 1

Chapter 1: What Is Organizational Culture? 3

Chapter 2: Principles Of Leadership 8

Chapter 3: A Key Virtue For Personal And Professional Success 24

Chapter 4: Importance Of Dependability In Fostering A Culture Of Trust And Collaboration 27

Chapter 6: How To Effectively Manage Your Time 41

Chapter 7: Time-Tracking On A Typical Day ... 43

Chapter 8: Be Truthful With Yourself 45

Chapter 9: Tactical Circumstances 60

Chapter 10: How To Determine Your Leadership Style And Develop Your Skills 65

Chapter 11: What Are Your Brand And Your Reputation? 71

Chapter 12: Roles Played By Mission And Vision 75

Chapter 13: Managing Expectations 80

Chapter 14: Communication 86

Chapter 15: What Makes A Good Leader 95

Chapter 16: Preparing For Leadership 101

Chapter 17: Developing The Right Attitude.. 112

Chapter 18: Spend On Yourself 117

Chapter 19: It Is Time To Assume Leadership 126

Chapter 20: Develop Personal Power Abilities 132

Chapter 21: Introduction Based On Positive Strengths 134

Chapter 22: The Evaluation Of Strength.......... 136

Chapter 24: Managing Your Free Time 137

Chapter 25: How Much Time Is Available? ... 139

Chapter 26: Clear Objectives Are Required .. 141

Chapter 29: Here Are Some Potential Consequences Of Ineffective Leadership: 146

Introduction

Individuals exercise leadership in their personal and professional lives. Individuals must acquire an understanding of the meaning and significance of leadership in order to implement this concept in an efficient and worthwhile manner. When they comprehend the concept's meaning and how it will assist them in performing their duties and achieving their objectives, they will put it into practice. The primary objective of the leaders is to provide their subordinates with the knowledge, support, and assistance they need to carry out their responsibilities in a well-organized and systematic manner, and to achieve the desired goals and objectives. When leaders carry out their responsibilities or collaborate with others, they must instill moral and ethical values and promote the well-being of all parties involved. In addition, the leaders must have a thorough understanding of the measures and approaches necessary to adapt to change, ensuring that they are effective and beneficial to both the members and the organization as a whole. Therefore, it can be stated that individuals in leadership positions must acquire a thorough comprehension of this concept prior to carrying out their duties. This research paper focuses on leadership and management, leadership functions, leadership types, and leadership roles.

Chapter 1: What Is Organizational Culture?

As with diversity, workplace culture influences performance, productivity, communication, recruitment, engagement, and retention, all of which determine the success of an organization. The work environment is comprised of attitudes, beliefs, and behaviors that constitute culture. A negative office culture will result in a toxic work environment and, eventually, failure. So, how do you create a workplace culture that encourages diverse ideas and places a premium on communication and collaboration?

Culture should be determined by the team rather than by the leader. One way to promote this is to find ways to improve the mood and concentration of your employees. Find ways to make employees happy through respectful communication and the cultivation of relationships based on mutual respect and trust. When employees come to you with suggestions and criticism, allow them to express themselves without silencing them or imposing negative consequences. Open communication fosters an atmosphere in which individuals feel heard, validated, respected, and trusted. This increases employee satisfaction and fosters a positive work environment.

You must also remember that people admire openness. Employees must believe that every aspect of the workplace is transparent. Employees are less likely to participate in workplace culture or communicate openly once they begin to suspect that there may be lying or cover-ups. This toxicity permeates your workplace and contributes to its negative culture.

If your employees are unhappy, they will not feel valued and will not have a sense of belonging to a community. Without a sense of community, openness, and happiness, employees are more likely to seek employment elsewhere, thereby decreasing your employee retention. Once an excessive number of team members leave, the workplace may feel less like a community, prompting others to leave as well. Continuously replacing employees is another way to lose your workplace community and team spirit, and you will either completely lose your workplace culture or be left with a culture that is constantly shifting and never materialises.

Employees who are content produce the highest quality work. If your workplace culture is negative, your employees will be dissatisfied, which will decrease employee output and quality, as well as your company's profits and reputation.

Sending out surveys that allow you to learn what kind of workplace culture your employees desire and how to provide it is a highly effective method for enhancing employee culture. Do you feel respected by your manager, your coworkers, and the organization? The questions "If there was one thing you could change about the organization, what would it be?" and "If there was one thing you could change about the organization, what would it be?" are excellent ways to determine how to create a culture that makes your team happy.

You can also symbolize your organization's values by printing them and distributing them to prospective and new employees. This way, they can become acquainted with these values prior to joining your company. You can do the same with the policies of your organization, including dress codes, training, and performance management.

Chapter 2: Principles of Leadership

Being able to persuade individuals with different worldviews towards a common objective can be quite laborious. For some, they devise a method to complete the task, ensuring their success. On what basis do they make decisions?

You recognise that humans are social beings. Effective leaders apply this proverb to their interactions with followers. Connecting with those beneath them enables them to assist others without expecting anything in return. As followers identify more with their leader, the effectiveness of this strategy depends more on the followers' psychology. So it appears that the leader is among them.

Unofficial loyalty is the emotional attachment that subordinates have for their superiors or leaders. In the majority of cases, they fear losing your support or friendship. This emphasises the significance of establishing emotional bonds, such as friendships, at every opportunity. You would then be able to deal with matters that appeal to you and your subordinates. After being told to do something, people will do it of their own volition because they feel they owe it to themselves.

Appeal Argument

It is essential to recognise that each individual acts in accordance with the values and beliefs closest to his or her heart. This determines whether we are under supervision. These are the indicators of our concealed values. To ensure that their loyalty is directed towards you, you must consider what would appeal to those beneath you.

Therefore, it is crucial that your objectives, intentions, and vision align with those of your most ardent supporters. This makes it easier for others to identify with you. The feeling of being one of them ensures a measure of loyalty.

Credence Principle

This principle pertains roughly to your communication and persuasion. If people are interested in your idea, you must have absolute confidence in the objectives and vision you are promoting. Certainty is instilled within us by trust. Therefore, this demonstrates that you can send mixed signals if you lack confidence. In most instances, trust inspires confidence in the organization's, group's, or team's direction or vision. We must demonstrate confidence through verbal and nonverbal communication.

Confidence is not limited to the visions you possess. Confidence in the skills and abilities of subordinates or followers is motivating to them. This gives them a sense of significance, particularly because they feel like they belong with you or fit in with your group. However, it would be necessary for you to establish the boundaries of this trust. You must recognise that excessive confidence can come across as arrogance, which has the opposite effect on people.

Principle of Compliance

The Principle of Harmony is effective because it is founded on the trust engendered by commitment. There will undoubtedly be occasions when you disagree with their argument. If we reject their arguments, they may end up distancing themselves from us.

You will undoubtedly not agree with all of your followers' points of view. To earn their trust, you must instil a degree of passivity. People only form relationships with those they deem trustworthy. Being dependable gives you an advantage over their resistance to your beliefs. However, this presents the challenge of striking a balance between their perspective and their perception of you.

The alignment considers the aspect of balancing everything in order to eliminate inconsistencies and, by extension, potential disagreements. This principle emphasises the significance of synchronising your speech and actions. When your actions match your words, it will be very easy for your followers to trust you because they will know what to anticipate. This gives them confidence, particularly if you've never been unreliable in the past.

Aligning your speech and actions with what motivates or attracts people in terms of their values is another application of the alignment principle. You recognise that it can be difficult to reconcile what you stand for with societal expectations. Nevertheless, it is always possible to fight for shared or common values.

Traction Concept

This principle entails fostering an environment in which people act of their own volition. When people make decisions based on their own discretion, motivation, or volition, they will direct the process with greater devotion. This principle is based on changing followers' perceptions of the world and making them want what they don't have in order to instil in them a desire to change things.

It is always easier to control people when they make their own decisions rather than when you force them to do so. However, it is crucial that you not only comprehend what they find desirable, but also how they make decisions.

Recognition Principle

For the majority of people, recognition is a crucial and rewarding component of any endeavour to achieve excellence. The ability to recognise, capitalise, and acknowledge an individual's contribution not only has a positive effect on the recognition process, but also reinforces the feeling of accomplishment. This element of recognition is essential for maintaining employee motivation and relevance in their respective contributions to the team, and it also encourages everyone to put forth their best effort to ensure the achievement of predetermined objectives.

The following are some ways in which we can express our appreciation for their contributions without creating undue fuss or commotion:

Awards - This is a common incentive used by many companies with a track record of success. This method of motivating team members has resulted in the successful attainment of predetermined goals for which the rewards are tangible rewards. Awards presented in a relatively public setting provide motivational factors that few other incentives can.

Bonuses - Bonuses are an additional method of recognising or rewarding the contributions of top performers. There are few things more persuasive than monetary compensation. This monetary incentive objective is pursued by the majority of high performers, so the use of monetary compensation is highly enticing and well worth the effort.

As recognition tools, effective reward systems, which may include travel incentives, freebies such as cars and tech "toys," and others, can be utilised. When the rewards are exclusive and one-of-a-kind, reflecting the significance of the contribution of the best person or top performer, the recognition becomes more enviable.

Promotions - Promotions are another effective means of recognising a superior person's contributions, as well as a means of promoting to others the esteem in which the person receiving the promotion is held.

Chapter 3: A Key Virtue for Personal and Professional Success

Many cultures and societies around the world place a high value on honesty and truthfulness. These characteristics are crucial for a variety of reasons:

When we are truthful with others, we are more likely to gain their trust and regard. This is particularly important in personal relationships, such as friendships and romantic relationships, as well as professional relationships.

Honesty promotes healthy relationships. When we are truthful with others, it is more likely that we will develop deep and meaningful relationships with them.

Personal integrity is bolstered by honesty, which is a necessary component of personal integrity. When we are honest and truthful, we are more likely to act according to our values and beliefs, which can make us feel good about ourselves and our actions.

Many people consider honesty to be a virtue and an essential characteristic of a good person. Being trustworthy, dependable, and fair are frequently associated with honesty and truthfulness.

Honesty is crucial to personal and professional success. When we are honest and truthful, others are more likely to respect and trust us, which can lead to advancement and success opportunities.

In conclusion, honesty and truthfulness are essential in all aspects of life, as they foster trust, respect, healthy relationships, personal integrity, and personal and professional success. In order to live a fulfilling and meaningful life, we must strive to be honest and forthright in all of our interactions with others.

Chapter 4: Importance of Dependability in Fostering a Culture of Trust and Collaboration

Dependability and honoring one's word can be advantageous in a variety of circumstances. Employees who consistently fulfil their responsibilities and keep their word are viewed as more dependable and competent. This may result in increased opportunities for career advancement and increased job satisfaction.

In order to build trust and strengthen friendships, dependability and commitment are crucial in interpersonal interactions. They are more likely to develop and maintain close relationships with those they can depend on to be there for them and keep their word.

Individuals and organisations that are dependable and honour their commitments can contribute to a culture of trust and cooperation at the societal level, which can have positive effects on numerous facets of social and economic life.

In terms of one's sense of self-worth and sense of accomplishment, following through on commitments and being dependable can boost one's self-respect. Additionally, it can help individuals develop a sense of responsibility and self-discipline, which can have a positive effect on their overall well-being.

Overall, the research indicates that dependability and commitment are advantageous in a variety of contexts and can have positive effects on both personal and professional relationships as well as on society as a whole.

Chapter 5: Conduct a Personal Evaluation

As a leader, you must develop yourself first. This chapter will discuss how to adopt a mindset of a leader. A personal evaluation of your beliefs and values will help us determine the most effective leadership style for you.

Development of leadership takes time. Schedules vary from individual to individual. Others will require additional time to refine their abilities.

Furthermore, even if you develop the fundamental frameworks of leadership, you will still need to improve over time. In the final chapter, we will examine leadership as an endless task. Now, let's get started so that you can become the leader you aspire to be.

Develop a leader's mentality

The mindset of a leader should emphasize growth in addition to a set of beliefs, attitudes, and expectations. Without the proper mindset, it may be impossible to be an effective leader.

Let's take a closer look at the following leadership qualities you must cultivate:

Do not be afraid of obstacles.

If you want to be a successful leader, you must face challenges without fear. Accept that obstacles are the norm and that you will face them frequently.

It is imperative that you have a strategy to defeat them. You will have access to individuals who can assist you when necessary.

Strive for a spirit of modesty

Even if you have confidence in your leadership skills, it is prudent to maintain humility. You should give credit whenever possible to those who deserve it. Take no credit for yourself and do not believe that you are superior to others.

In addition to accepting that you may be mistaken about something, you want to acknowledge what you may have misunderstood. You should avoid assigning blame whenever possible. Self-responsibility can take you very far.

Just make a choice.

Leadership requires no hesitation. They must decide now, as time is not on their side in the future. When it comes to being decisive, you shouldn't second-guess yourself.

The more information you have, the better decision you will be able to make. Whenever you require this information, obtain it as soon as possible. A decisive leader will be admired regardless of the time remaining.

Become an innovative leader

Every leader must be able to think creatively outside of the box. It makes them adaptable in terms of finding solutions to particular problems.

Due to their resourcefulness, a leader will have the confidence to assist their team in overcoming obstacles. They will have access to a wealth of information that will aid them in answering questions.

Become a "thinker of the future"

The ability to anticipate will enable leaders to make the best decisions. These individuals are "future thinkers." Things could alter at any moment.

A capable leader will be adaptable in the face of change. Change and last-minute alterations are characteristics of a growth mindset. Fixed perspectives, not so much.

People with a growth mindset are proactive and plan ahead. Fixed mindsets lack foresight and fly in the dark, hoping not to crash.

Credible and genuine

You should be honest with the people you hire to help you achieve your business goals. You need them to be aware of what lies ahead.

When answering questions, you should be straightforward and truthful. People will lose trust in you and possibly leave if you lie.

A dependable leader adheres to honesty to the greatest extent possible. Sincerity is always the best practise.

Yes, they deserve honour and respect

Leaders must recognize and acknowledge individuals who have achieved success on their own.

Through the efforts of their subordinates, they achieved a goal or overcame a difficulty. They were one step closer to achieving what could have been a significant objective (like sales).

A leader is successful in and of themselves. However, they will defer to and acknowledge their subordinates. Moreover, they can reward them if they perform well.

Who is accountable? Really?

You accept responsibility for any undesirable outcomes. Do not attribute your problems to others. Find a way to make the 'wrong' right if necessary.

It is in our nature to make errors. You are not a machine but a human leader. There will be times when you are incorrect, even if you believe you are correct.

What kind of leader are you?

This section will identify the leadership style that works best for you. You will be able to identify your personal beliefs and values based on these leaders' defining characteristics. Here are examples of various styles:

Autocratic Administration

These leaders are more of the "my way or the highway" variety. They have the last word. They will be less likely to be receptive to ideas, conversations, or anything else. Consequently, a team member's contribution may go unheard.

When they implement new policies, no prior notice is given. If you are in a small group or work in an industry such as the military or government, you can employ this strategy. In the majority of business environments, this may not work well.

The Democratic Chairman

Despite your authority over day-to-day operations, you involve your team in the majority of decision-making.

Obviously, you will be unable to perform this action during an emergency (where you can be a bit autocratic). Your team members will, however, have the opportunity to share their ideas and thoughts.

Moreover, they can influence crucial business decisions. If all ideas are presented, the majority will vote for the most appropriate alternative. The decision will be implemented in accordance with the outcomes.

Style of transformational leadership

A transformational leader is among the most successful types of leaders. They are powerful because they give their teams autonomy. In addition, they are visionaries eager to implement their own ideas.

It is frequently combined with certain types of leadership, particularly those that seek positive change.

The Official

A diplomatic leader's objective is to make everyone happy. To ensure that everyone gets what they want, negotiations may be required. Such leaders can easily solve problems (even complex ones).

The Official

A company will have a command structure. The chief executive is the highest authority. Below the top leader will be additional leaders, each with their own hierarchy.

The military has a similar organisational structure. In the business world, the CEO may have ultimate authority over company matters, but subordinate leaders will always report to the regional manager (e.g., a branch manager).

Style of Transactional Leadership

This type of leader will reward those who perform well and punish those who perform poorly. Sports are an excellent analogy. A star athlete on a cold streak must be benched until they improve.

When the star athlete performs well, regardless of whether they are a starter or a reserve, they receive more playing time. The same holds true in business.

Keep track of who is productive and who may be hindering your progress.

It takes time to develop leadership skills. You will also be able to determine your leadership style. Creating a mentality will be one of the most difficult aspects of your development process.

In any circumstance, you can be confident in your ability to make the right decisions, give credit to your team, and accept responsibility for your errors. Let's move on to discussing some of your most important leadership responsibilities.

Chapter 6: How to Effectively Manage Your Time

Time management is the process of planning and organising how you divide your time among various tasks. People and society are driven by productivity, and if we all practise efficient time management, we can all become more productive. Planning your time enables you to make the most efficient use of it and complete the necessary tasks. Time management is essential in all aspects of life. Here are some benefits: If you manage your time effectively, you will be more productive and efficient, experience less stress, and have a greater chance of achieving important life and career goals.

Inadequate time management can have severe consequences, such as missed deadlines. ineffective work process low fundamental value and increased strain If you want to pass your driver's licence exam, you should schedule time for studying theory and taking driving lessons with your instructor, as these activities will help you achieve your goal. You can manage your time primarily in two ways: by creating to-do lists and by using a time-based approach. Personally, I utilise a combination of both. I enjoy planning my weekly schedule by creating time blocks in Google Calendar and then creating daily to-do lists.

Chapter 7: Time-tracking on a typical day

Before you develop better time management skills. You must first recognize how you manage your time. Ask yourself immediately, "What am I doing wrong?" so you can pinpoint exactly what you are doing wrong. Then ask yourself, "Where are you spending your time?" To answer this question, I suggest keeping time logs. If you're anything like me and spend the majority of your day on your computer or phone, I'd recommend looking at your screen time report because it should give you a good idea of how you spend your time. It will display the amount of time you spend on specific apps and categories such as productivity and entertainment. Personally, I prefer to track my time using an app on my Smartphone. You can also track your time using a piece of paper or a post-it note. Keeping track of your time may appear tedious or unnecessary, but once you start doing it, you'll see all the benefits.

Chapter 8: Be truthful with yourself

Occasionally, I sit down to study for about three minutes before becoming distracted and watching YouTube for three hours. However, admitting to yourself that you procrastinated for three hours is not a particularly pleasant experience, so you often convince yourself that you are studying and being productive. However, when you are tracking your time and creating a time log, please be completely honest. If you include four hours of Netflix watching in your time log, you will feel bad and embarrassed. However, when you add four hours of productive time to your time log, you will feel accomplished and good about yourself. This is exactly what you want, as your brain will realise that being productive is more rewarding and feels better than watching Netflix and wasting time.

Set objectives and priorities

I am aware that you often have multiple goals or objectives you wish to achieve, but you must realise that you cannot do everything. Therefore, you must choose specific objectives or priorities and determine what is most important to you at this time. Therefore, you will know precisely what you should be working towards. You should set goals on a weekly or monthly basis. Consequently, you can stay on track and ensure that your goals are always visible and in front of your face so that you never forget them.

Tip 4: Limit your time spent on tasks that aren't essential.

For instance, if you want to spend more quality time with your friends and family and get better grades in school, watching

Netflix for four or five hours per day will not help you achieve these goals, so you should limit the amount of time you spend watching Netflix. I accomplish this by placing restrictions on specific applications on my various devices. If you're an Apple user, this functionality is built-in; if you're an Android user, I'm sure you can download apps that provide the same functionality. If the tasks you wish to limit are non-digital and more creative, such as reading a fictional book or drawing, I would suggest setting a timer and, when it goes off, doing your best to return to your work and be productive rather than doing things you don't really need to be doing.

Find the optimal planning technique

Planning is essential for time management so that you know what you should be doing and when; there is little decision-making involved. However, you must find the method of planning that works best for you. There are various options, such as having a to-do list, which is what I prefer to do. However, for those who need a bit more structure in their day, I recommend hourly planning, where you know exactly what you need to be doing at specific hours of the day, or weekly planning, which can be quite helpful. You can also experiment with different planning methods, such as bullet journaling, planning everything digitally on your computer, or using a paper planner with pre-designed layouts. There are also various time management strategies, such as time blocking and batching. One of my favourites is batching, which involves performing similar tasks in succession. I established a rule in which I devote a specific day of the week to a particular subject; for example, I study math on Mondays. Having physics on Tuesdays, web development and programming on Thursdays, and revision on Fridays gives your week a lot of structure and helps you remain productive.

Tip 6 - Examine

Perform a weekly review of the past week and reflect on what transpired, how it transpired, and everything else. Thus, you can identify the mistakes you made this week so you don't repeat them next week, and this can also serve as a source of inspiration and motivation because you can track your progress week by week. You test out new strategies and plan ways to improve, and I'm not sure what that means for you, but it makes me feel tremendously encouraged and motivated.

Set a limit on your to-do list and avoid adding too many tasks.

With 20 items on your to-do list, it is likely that you will become overwhelmed and refuse to begin. Instead, I would suggest setting three daily priorities. These three items should not be minuscule, but rather one- or two-hour projects. This strategy works so well because you focus on your priorities first, and then at the end of the day you can complete bonus tasks or small tasks that are not as important. However, they will not distract you from the primary objectives you had for the day.

Know when to multitask and when not to multitask.

Remember how I used to simultaneously study and watch YouTube videos? This is an example of multitasking that is actually quite bad, and you shouldn't do it because, oftentimes, you won't be able to concentrate on your study material when an interesting show is playing in the background. Nevertheless, there are other productive ways to multitask, such as listening to an audio book while cleaning, doing laundry, or performing other household tasks. This will be productive because one of the tasks will not necessarily distract you from the other, and you can complete both tasks simultaneously. The fact that you are simultaneously reading a book and performing another task ends up saving you time. My favourite feature is the ability to exchange an audiobook for a different one if you decide you don't enjoy it.

Tip 9 - take breaks

When you've been doing something for a while, it's often necessary to unwind and relax for a while. You will be more focused and productive if you take a short break and then return to the task at hand. However, you should be careful not to take a two-hour break after only ten minutes of work, as this will have no positive effect on your productivity during breaks. Frequently, I enjoy grabbing a quick snack or listening to music. My mood is significantly improved by a brief bout of dancing.

Never over-schedule your day

Nothing takes significantly longer than anticipated, and random tasks arise that require immediate attention. There may be pressing matters or you may suddenly feel exhausted, requiring you to take some time to relax and regain your energy; this is perfectly normal. Always leave some wiggle room in your schedule, and remember that you're not a work machine and shouldn't be working nonstop. Remember that productivity is all about completing tasks more quickly and efficiently so that you have more time for yourself and the activities you enjoy. It's not all about working; keep this in mind, as many people tend to forget.

The Importance of Verbal Communication

Words matter beyond the straightforward exchange of data. Style and tone of delivery can also affect what is said and how the audience perceives the information.

Developing the ability to speak clearly and concisely in person and over the phone is a crucial skill for any leader. In addition, a good leader should understand the distinction between the two and other factors that contribute to communication besides the words and phrases used.

Eye to eye Correspondence

Face-to-face communication is one of the most effective means of conveying ideas and initiating dialogue. However, it may not be the most effective method for conveying detailed information. Understanding the distinction between the two is frequently the difference between success and failure when planning new activities and initiatives.

For instance, it's ideal to be able to communicate face-to-face, but a hurried conversation as you pass by someone's desk is not an effective method for ensuring that things will be completed accurately. A traditional meeting or an email would be the best option.

Non-verbal communication

Your nonverbal communication will reveal a great deal about your identity and your correspondence style. Additionally, thoughtless nonverbal communication can undermine the message you intended to convey. In the event that your non-verbal communication does not match your spoken words, there can be a significant disconnect that can be confusing or suggest to others that you are not being honest or are in that state of mind.

For instance, if you speak and listen with your arms crossed in front of your chest, this could convey negative messages. Your audience may believe you are guarded, angry, or impartial, particularly if you do not look at them or turn to the side.

Additionally, collapsed arms indicate that others should avoid you. They could attempt to demonstrate determination or refusal, so that individuals would likely never ask for what they need because your nonverbal communication is already apparently telling them no.

Act Regular

When interacting with individuals face-to-face, a more relaxed and natural body position with your arms dangling freely at your sides is a considerably more inviting stance.

While conversing, make every effort to avoid playing. Practice quietness. Keep in contact. If you are in a large gathering, you should survey the space. Try not to pace, but feel free to move around as needed. While listening, make head gestures. Listen attentively Try not to initiate conversation. Wait until the individual has concluded.

Then, repeat what you believe to be the essence of the question, in the event that no one has heard and to ensure you have heard correctly.

Modality of speech

In spoken correspondence, both face-to-face and particularly over the telephone, tone of voice plays a significant role. For example, if expressed at the beginning of the gathering, the phrase "Thank you for joining us" could sound sincere and beautiful. However, if it is said to a person who is arriving shortly late with an emphasis on "Thank you," it can appear to be sarcastic or even inconsiderate.

In essence, "Much obliged" conveys different meanings when spoken versus when it is written.

Typically, it is an expression of gratitude, though it may also be witty. Communication style is vital.

Assisting with Gatherings and Introductions

If you are a business leader, you will occasionally be responsible for meetings and introductions. This could be the moment of truth for your reputation as a decent person.

pioneer. Your initiative will not be questioned on the off chance that you are a sorted out pioneer with a clear strategy and the capacity to direct a gathering in a way that will yield certain results.

In the event that things deteriorate into unpredictable, volatile conflicts and no work is completed, these meetings will produce no dependable results and tarnish your reputation as a strong leader.

As far as presentation, such as PowerPoint decks, numerous organisations today live and die by their decks. Consequently, it is essential to hone this ability so you can make and deliver introductions that maintain interest, persuade, and enlighten, rather than bore the audience to sleep.

Chapter 9: Tactical Circumstances

Currently, many individuals have misconceptions. No reasonable person would mistake the executive for a father, a therapist, or even a personnel director. His interest can and should be completely objective and non-political. "This has nothing to do with you," he might tell the employee. Everyone in your position would receive the same treatment. As long as you continue to work for me, I will provide you with ample opportunities to realise your full potential. My job entails fostering your growth and contentment. The sooner you become a significant contributor to this organisation, the better. If you can perform your duties in a more efficient manner, please do so; if something is preventing you from doing so, please discuss the matter with me. Upon being correct, you will

Receive my full support as well as the recognition you merit.

There will be no genuine growth in an employee without instruction. Regularly, the superior must be aware of the successes and failures of the subordinate, and he must ensure that the subordinate is also aware of these outcomes. At this point in the evaluation, a particularly challenging aspect of leadership becomes apparent. How can criticism be objective and still be effective? How can a decision or method be critiqued without making the employee feel personally insulted?

At the current time, effective communication is crucial for two reasons. In addition to long-term damage to employee morale, a very specific short-term effect is the employee's failure to do what he should to implement the boss's alternative plan, because its failure may prove that he was correct in the first place. It is all too easy for a leader to incite hostility and defensiveness by approaching a problem impersonally and disregarding the human emotions and motivations at play.

Surprisingly, such failures appear to occur more frequently in the workplace than elsewhere, and we may well wonder if we haven't isolated management behaviour from behaviour outside the workplace, such as in the home. We do not believe that an order or memorandum is the most effective means of communicating our desires at home.

Most reasonably intelligent individuals learn early in life how to persuade others to cooperate. It comes naturally to create a personal and emotional environment that is appropriate for the individual (e.g., spouse, adult son, adolescent daughter, or child) and the specific request.

In the workplace, we don the mask of an employer or executive and set aside our innate human relations skills.

Plus, we are likely to know which aspects of, say, a vacation plan to highlight in order to make it appealing to a wife who wants to be served, a son who wants to fish, or a daughter who wants adolescent companions.

We may also discover that one of them will be more receptive to persuasion if she has a say in the decision-making process, whereas the other would prefer to be presented with a completed plan for his approval or disapproval. Indeed, we likely react to such differences at home without much consideration.

At work, however, we don the persona of an executive or employer and set aside our normal human relations intuition. We attempt to manage our tasks by issuing impersonal orders or directives to whoever is in charge of carrying them out, oblivious to the fact that effective human resource mobilisation requires everyone's voluntary participation. Leadership is interaction with others. It requires a leader who knows how to use them, as well as followers with particular qualities and skills.

Chapter 10: How to Determine Your Leadership Style and Develop Your Skills

Each individual has a unique leadership style, and there is no single best way to lead. In reality, the majority of people are a combination of multiple leadership styles, depending on the situation or the person they are leading. Nevertheless, it can be useful to determine which of these styles feels most natural to you so that you can learn how to improve your skills in areas where you feel weak or where you need to develop. By determining your personal leadership style, you can establish clear goals and standards for self-improvement, as well as determine the type of environment that will be most conducive to your style.

The Five Elements

To determine your leadership style, you must do more than answer a few yes-or-no questions. It involves examining multiple facets of your life, assessing how you behave in each circumstance, and determining which aspects are most important to you. Once you are aware of this, it is easier to evaluate potential work situations through the same lenses and determine whether they align with your priorities.

Visionary and idealistic - This trait entails seeing opportunities where others do not. You're able to envision a desirable future state for an organisation or project, and then persuade others to join you. People with high visionary/idealistic scores are typically visionary, optimistic, and energising leaders who can inspire those around them. They also tend to be excellent at generating new ideas, but struggle with implementation and execution due to a lack of follow-through skills.

2. Affiliative: As an affiliative leader, you are primarily concerned with fostering relationships and preserving harmony within your team or organisation as a whole. You excel at encouraging collaboration and working with others to achieve shared objectives. People with a high affiliation score tend to be empathetic leaders who are skilled at resolving conflicts and ensuring that their teams work well together. They have a tendency to be extremely people-oriented, which can sometimes hinder

their decision-making because they care more about being liked than respected.

This component focuses on creating opportunities for others to contribute ideas, opinions, and suggestions, and then implementing those ideas that you believe will benefit all parties involved in a project or business endeavour. People who score highly in democratic leadership tend to be excellent at empowering their teams and fostering teamwork. They are frequently highly creative leaders who can generate new ideas and implement them once they have been decided. As a result of requiring input from all parties involved prior to moving forward with plans, they may occasionally struggle to make decisions.

4. Commanding/authoritative - As a commanding leader, you are primarily concerned with getting things done effectively and efficiently, which frequently necessitates making snap decisions without regard for what others may think. High scorers on commanding leadership are typically decisive leaders with strong problem-solving skills and the ability to make difficult decisions when necessary. They are excellent at coming up with creative solutions to problems, but they can sometimes appear intimidating or overbearing because they do not seek the opinions of others prior to making decisions.

5. Pacesetting/Controlling - This element focuses on motivating your team by establishing challenging goals that push everyone out of their comfort zones and toward excellence. High scorers on pacesetting leadership tend

to be highly motivated leaders who enjoy pushing themselves and their teams to achieve more than they believed possible prior to beginning a new project or business venture.

Chapter 11: WHAT ARE YOUR BRAND AND YOUR REPUTATION?

One of the most important differences between your brand and your reputation is that you have some control over your brand. However, the majority of your reputation is determined by external factors. I don't mean that you can't affect your reputation; however, if your branding is inconsistent, it will undoubtedly have an effect. Your reputation is dependent on how effectively you convey your brand image to customers and employees.

As your potential and current employees are also a part of your brand, you must ensure that they are familiar with you. Using feedback mechanisms and surveys, you can determine if your current employees are aligned with your brand and mission. These surveys should be kept anonymous so that your employees can provide candid feedback without fear of repercussions. You can also conduct one-on-one sessions with your team to determine what they like and dislike about the workplace. You can also conduct these surveys in educational institutions (where your future talent pool is forming) to gain an objective understanding of your organization's strengths and weaknesses.

The next step is difficult because you are likely to have a preference for the organisation or team for which you work. However, you must consider the working conditions within your organisation and team, as well as how these conditions influence performance. This serves two purposes. First, you gain an understanding of the team's core values. Does your team, for instance, prioritise individualism over collaboration? Does it prioritise creativity over conformity? How does your team respond to uncertainty and pressure? Does it generate more effective solutions for structured or unstructured problems? You may not agree with all the responses, but you will likely have a clear understanding of what you actually believe (rather than what you want to).

You now have the chance to close any gaps between your vision and the actual world. If you want your team to be more focused on innovation, you must make the necessary adjustments. Likewise, if you wish to foster a more collaborative culture within your team, you must take the necessary steps.

An EVP is the reason a potential employee chooses your organisation over others. This should be a concise statement outlining what you can offer the candidate. This includes not only monetary and other benefits, but also the job description, development and mentorship opportunities, and perhaps even a sense of where they can see themselves in the company over the next few years. The ideal employee value proposition (EVP) should be a combination of tangible and intangible benefits that employees receive when they join your team.

Chapter 12: ROLES PLAYED BY MISSION AND VISION

A mission statement describes the organization's raison d'être and how it intends to serve its key constituents. Customers, employees, and investors are the most frequently mentioned stakeholders, but government and communities (in the form of social or environmental impact) can also be mentioned. Typically, mission statements are more extensive than vision statements. Occasionally, mission statements also include a summary of the organization's core values. The emotionally invested beliefs of an individual or group, in this case the organisation, are its values.

In contrast, a vision statement is a forward-looking declaration of an organization's objectives and aspirations. In many ways, the mission statement describes the "reason for being" of the organisation, whereas the vision statement describes the organization's desired future state. The strategy should derive directly from the vision, as its purpose is to realise the vision and fulfil the organization's mission. Typically, vision statements are brief in length.

To reiterate, mission statements are typically longer than vision statements because they communicate an organization's fundamental values. Mission statements provide the answers to the questions "Who are we?" and "What do we value as an organisation?" Vision statements are typically concise, future-focused statements. Vision statements, for instance, answer the question "Where is this organization headed?"

On the other hand, organizations also include value statements that either reaffirm or explicitly state the organization's values that may not be apparent in the mission or vision statements.

Mission and vision statements serve three essential functions: (1) communicate the organization's purpose to its stakeholders, (2) inform strategy development, and (3) establish the measurable goals and objectives that will be used to evaluate the success of the organization's strategy.

First, mission and vision serve as a vehicle for communicating the purpose and values of an organization to all of its key stakeholders. Stakeholders are influential parties with a vested interest in the organization's future. Employees, customers, investors, suppliers, and institutions such as governments are important stakeholders. Typically, these statements would be widely disseminated and frequently discussed in order for their meaning to be broadly understood, shared, and internalized. The greater an organization's employees' understanding of its mission and vision, the greater their ability to comprehend its strategy and its implementation.

Second, mission and vision provide a target for the development of strategy. Thus, one criterion of a good strategy is the extent to which it assists the organisation in achieving its mission and vision. Sometimes it is helpful to visualise mission, vision, and strategy as a funnel in order to comprehend their relationship. At the widest point of the funnel, you will find the mission statement's inputs. In the narrower portion of the funnel, you will find the vision statement, which is a condensed version of the mission that can guide the development of the strategy. In the narrowest portion of the funnel, you will find the strategy, which specifies what the company will do and will not do to achieve its vision. Additionally, vision statements serve as a link between the mission and the strategy. In this sense, the most effective vision statements generate tension and restlessness regarding the status quo; that is, they should foster a spirit of continuous innovation and improvement.

Thirdly, the mission and vision provide a high-level guide, while the strategy provides a specific guide, to the goals and objectives that demonstrate the success or failure of the strategy and the achievement of the mission's larger set of stated objectives.

CHAPTER 13: MANAGING EXPECTATIONS

We will begin by discussing the significance of establishing clear expectations and how to do so in a way that ensures everyone is aligned and working towards the same goals. We will also examine the role of communication in managing expectations, as well as how to communicate effectively with your team and stakeholders to avoid misunderstandings and conflicts.

The purpose of this article is to provide you with a solid understanding of how to effectively manage expectations in a manner that reduces stress and boosts productivity. With this foundation in place, you will be well-equipped to face the upcoming challenges and achieve success with your project or endeavour.

Avoiding Overcommitment and Burnout through Realistic Expectations

For the success of any endeavour or project, it is crucial to establish reasonable goals. By establishing lucid, attainable goals and objectives, you can ensure that everyone is on the same page and working towards the same outcome. However, it is essential to avoid overcommitment and burnout by setting realistic and attainable goals.

Here are some suggestions for establishing reasonable expectations:

Before setting expectations, it is essential to have a thorough understanding of your budget, personnel, and any other constraints. This will assist you in setting reasonable and realisable goals within the constraints of your resources.

It is essential to prioritise tasks and prioritise the most important ones first. By concentrating on the most important tasks, you can maximise your resources and ensure you're making progress toward your objectives.

Communicate effectively: Clear and efficient communication is essential for setting reasonable expectations. Ensure that your team is involved in the goal-setting process, and promote open and honest communication to prevent misunderstandings and conflicts.

Plan for contingencies: Regardless of how well you plan, unforeseen obstacles will always arise. It is essential to incorporate contingencies and flexibility into your project plan to account for potential obstacles.

These tips will assist you in setting reasonable goals, avoiding overcommitment and burnout, and increasing your likelihood of success.

Setting realistic expectations has a number of benefits for both the project's success and the team members' well-being. Here are several significant effects of setting reasonable expectations:

When members of a team feel overburdened and stressed, their morale can suffer. By establishing reasonable expectations, you can help team members feel more confident and competent, thereby boosting team morale.

When expectations are unrealistic, team members may become demotivated and lose concentration. By establishing reasonable expectations, you can keep your team motivated and productive.

High levels of stress and burnout can result in high employee turnover, which can be costly and disruptive to the project. By setting reasonable expectations, you can reduce burnout and increase employee retention.

When expectations are unrealistic, there is a greater likelihood that the project will fail. By setting reasonable expectations, you can increase your likelihood of success and accomplish your objectives.

For the success of any endeavour or project, it is crucial to establish reasonable goals. By doing so, you can increase team morale, productivity, retention, and your chances of achieving success.

Chapter 14: Communication

Communication is the demonstration or interaction of utilising words, sounds, signs, or ways of behaving to communicate or trade data or to communicate your thoughts, considerations, sentiments, and so forth, to another person.

No matter how you look at it, it is one of the most important communication skills we all need to develop and hone throughout our careers. "Communicating information and ideas" is consistently regarded as one of the most essential skills for pioneers seeking long-term success. Communication is also embedded in other leadership abilities and skills, such as "driving agents," "participative leadership," and "building and patching connections."

Without being an exceptional communicator, it is very difficult to become an extraordinary leader. I want to believe that you noticed the previous sentence did not imply that you are an exceptional speaker - a stark contrast. Rarely can the path to becoming a gifted communicator be found in what has been demonstrated in the realm of academia. We are prepared to focus on articulation, jargon, presence, conveyance, punctuation, sentence structure, etc. from our earliest days in the homeroom.

At the conclusion of each day, we are instructed to concentrate on ourselves. Leaders urgently need to learn the more unpretentious aspects of correspondence (those that focus on others), which are rarely emphasised in the classroom. In the following section, I will discuss a few communication traits that, when utilised consistently, will assist you in achieving better communication outcomes.

Leadership starts with effective communication. Effective communication is clear, direct, and tailored to the recipient. A decent leader will get some margin to figure out which communication style and technique (message, email, telephone or face to face) turn out best for each colleague. By communicating with your group, you create a culture of trust, compatibility, and shared responsibility. Communicate frequently, clearly, and truthfully.

Effective communication is essential for building trust, adjusting efforts in pursuit of goals, and effecting positive change. When there is a lack of communication, significant data can be misinterpreted, causing connections to persist and, eventually, impeding progress.

If you're interested in enhancing your leadership abilities, here are eight relational skills that will make you more effective at work. Essential skills of persuasive communicator:

1. compassion

Sympathy. The capacity to share another's emotions and thoughts. The highest level of listening. You must not only listen and comprehend what someone says, but also comprehend how they feel.

In terms of leadership, empathy is not merely a nice-to-have; it is essential for establishing trust, certainty, and commitment among your team.

Sympathy is the capacity to perceive and relate to the thoughts and experiences of others. Leaders who operate from a place of compassion, understanding, and empathy establish more stable relationships among their representatives and enhance execution in all cases.

2. undivided consideration

The most compelling leaders understand when to speak and, more importantly, when to listen. Request employees' opinions, thoughts, and criticism to demonstrate that you care. In addition, when they do share, effectively contribute to the discussion by suggesting conversation starters, encouraging them to elaborate, and taking notes.

It is essential to observe silence and refrain from interfering. Maintain your focus on the speaker and what they are saying. In addition, you must eliminate any interruptions, such as your wireless's constant pings or the display of approaching messages.

3. forthrightness

By communicating openly about the organization's objectives, amazing opportunities, and challenges, leaders can build trust among their group and foster an environment where employees feel encouraged to share their ideas and collaborate. Simply acknowledging errors can empower trial and error and provide a haven for dynamic critical thinking.

Each individual must comprehend the contribution they make to the organization's success. The more transparent leaders are, the easier it is for representatives to follow them.

4. Lucidity

While conversing with representatives, be specific. Define the ideal outcome of a project or major initiative and be clear about what you want to see accomplished at the conclusion of each accomplishment. If objectives are not being met, consider refining your message or asking how you can provide additional clarity or assistance.

The greater your clarity, the less confusion will be associated with your needs. Representatives will comprehend their objectives and feel more engaged as a result.

5. Open non-verbal communication

To ensure you are conveying the intended message, focus on your nonverbal communication. If you are attempting to motivate someone, speaking with clenched fists and a furrowed brow will not send the right message. Engage visually to demonstrate interest and compatibility, and flash a genuine smile to convey warmth and confidence.

How could leaders build confidence in Communication? Consistency. Express aloud whatever you will incessantly bring about. Ensure your messages are consistent with your words and actions. Like clockwork, continually. Demonstrating that you are solid and dependable is a simple and effective way to build trust with your employees.

▫ Character. Being a good person and making the best choice. Be accountable and admit your mistakes. When you demonstrate how to do something, your representatives will adhere to this pattern.

Perspicacity. Clarify and condense your examination of strategies and objectives in all correspondence with representatives. Always be practical and never overpromise what you cannot deliver.

▫ Coordination of effort Requesting employee input demonstrates that you value the criticism and evaluations of others. By remembering them for the interaction, but using their thoughts, you build long-term trust and loyalty while incorporating them into the arrangement.

⬚ Mindful. Deny discussed the significance of empathy and compassion in the video. Demonstrate your concern for others by acknowledging their emotions and concerns.

CHAPTER 15: What Makes A Good Leader

From clear correspondence to regard for others, cultivating these traits can help you supervise more effectively — at every level.

The importance of the world's speedy, innovation-driven areas of strength is greater now than at any time in recent memory. Regardless, what characteristics make a good leader? Moreover, how does effective leadership influence the working environment? Some of the responses, such as avoiding prevalence problems and advancing your education through an administration degree programme, may surprise you.

They communicate plainly.

Dealing with a group, especially in the workplace, begins with excellent correspondence. Whether they are writing an email or delivering face-to-face criticism, great leaders always say out loud what they intend to say. They are neither latently aggressive nor avoid addressing problems immediately.

They are enthusiastic about their work.

Numerous great leaders are unafraid to express their passion for their work. Obviously, you can still be an effective leader even if your professional and personal interests are not a perfect match. Consider what you appreciate most about your work, and cultivate your enthusiasm for that — you may discover that you're guiding yourself toward greater workplace fulfilment.

They could not care less about their notoriety.

In fact, you may be less effective if your primary concern is whether or not everyone likes you. Whether it's providing in-depth analysis or bringing up a training you believe is unreliable, learning to be a good leader means deciding to do or say what is best for your team and organisation, even if it makes you temporarily uncomfortable.

They keep their minds active.

Remaining receptive to innovative ideas. Instead of opposing change, exceptional leaders are adaptable and versatile. They are receptive and welcome hypotheses that differ from their own.

They work for their elected officials.

Great leaders recognise that their primary responsibility is to ensure that their subordinates have the resources and support they need to perform their duties as proficiently and effectively as possible, and to flourish in the workplace.

They are encouraging and empowering. Excellent leaders are motivating. On the off chance that there are lapses in execution, they have some leeway to coach and prepare the employee. In all types of adversity, great leaders inspire their followers to be their absolute best by empowering them to do so.

They respect others.

From direct reports and colleagues to clients and superiors, great leaders treat others as they would wish to be treated. Those they lead frequently adhere to this pattern, resulting in more grounded decisions throughout the workplace.

They construct connections.

A vital characteristic of a good leader is the ability to form beneficial relationships. The integrity of dependable administrators cannot be compromised by others. Instead of protecting their region, they are continually building bridges with others. A good leader understands the value of commonly useful connections and actively seeks them out.

They instruct others in proper procedure.

The best supervisors recognise that setting a good example is a crucial component of being a good leader. Great leaders demonstrate they are willing to do anything they would ask of their employees, from putting in extra hours on a significant task to approaching others with deference and generosity.

They continuously acquire new knowledge.

Perhaps the most important quality of effective leaders is that they are perpetual students. They prioritise their education, whether through traditional means such as constructing their skills through administration degree programmes or through everyday consideration of various divisions and jobs. Generally, a decent leader must acquire more knowledge.

Consider an online business the board degree if you're a good manager who wants to become a great manager but lacks the time and energy to complete a management degree programme. Authorized online schools and colleges are designed for working professionals, allowing them to pursue administration degree programmes while balancing work and family obligations.

Chapter 16: Preparing for Leadership

Since biblical times, the Bible recounts tales of women from diverse backgrounds who assumed leadership roles. Women such as Deborah led armies to victory. Queen Esther, who ultimately saved her people by risking her life. Ruth, a foreigner in the eyes of the Israelites, eventually became the great-grandmother of King David and entered the lineage of Jesus. Anna, who spoke for God in the temple, was among the first leaders to recognise Jesus as the Messiah. Lydia was an accomplished businesswoman. Dorcas, who made a living with a needle and thread while serving the poor. Priscilla, who taught and mentored other leaders. And countless others.

In recent times, countless women have responded to God's call and assumed positions of leadership. Some took bold steps. Some cautiously. And some with fear. Amy Carmichael, Corrie ten Boom, Elisabeth Elliot, Joni Eareckson Tada, Mother Teresa, Rosa Parks, and Ruth Bell Graham are examples of influential women. Alternatively, women such as Elinor Young, Helen Roseveare, Henrietta Mears, and Faye Edgerton. Some are household names, while others are less well-known.

Some women confronted disappointment with bravery and resolve. Women like Mary McLeod Bethune, whose goal was to become an African missionary. When she was informed that there were no openings for "Negro missionaries" in Africa, she recalled saying, "Africans in America required Christ and education just as much as Negroes in Africa... My life's work was accomplished in my own country, not in Africa." Mary's accomplishments ranged from founding schools and hospitals to serving as president of Bethune-Cookman College, founder of the National Council of Negro Women, and special adviser to three presidents of the United States, among others. 3

Some women were intent on following their own path until God revealed otherwise. Dr. Ida Scudder vowed never to follow in her family's footsteps as missionaries. Upon ceasing her struggle with God, she enrolled in medical school and returned to India, where she was born. There, she cared for female patients and educated Indian women to become physicians and nurses. She grew a single-bed dispensary into one of India's largest and most prestigious medical facilities. 4

There are numerous generations of women whose stories deserve to be told, but to do so would require numerous additional books. Some women made an impact in their local communities, while others had a global impact. Many had modest beginnings and overcame tremendous obstacles. The majority, if not all, of their tales led them down paths they never could have imagined.

Today is no exception. Each of us has a story that includes sorrow, happiness, illness, defeat, confusion, adventure, betrayal, and victory. It is all present. We may be in business, ministry, politics, the arts, or advocacy. We may serve our country or another nation. God directs and sustains those whom he has called. The only thing he asks is that we stand obediently in the spot he created us to fill in history. Each of us will likely take a different route to get there, but he always knows the path we must take to bring him glory.

As I continue to share the story of God's patience and faithfulness in my life to date, I pray that God will uplift you through his mercy, empower you through his grace, and encourage you through the hope that he alone can provide.

Before we conclude this first section, Anchored in Hope, let's examine five essential leadership principles for those just beginning their incredible journey.

Be Intrigued

As a child, I asked many questions. When I was unable to obtain answers from the adults in my life, I found them in a book. Typically, this entailed a walk to the bookmobile, which visited outlying communities without a public library. It stopped every few weeks at the intersection of our street and the main road. There, I awaited my turn to enter the small bus that had been converted into a library by standing in line. Oh, I absolutely adored that mobile library!

The driver, who was also the librarian, motioned me in when it was my turn. I would ascend a few steps and enter a bookstore where books lined every interior wall, leaving barely room for two customers. I enjoyed times when there were few people in line and I could peruse the shelves leisurely in search of intriguing books. If the item I sought was unavailable, I would submit a request and the librarian would bring alternatives on the next run.

But being curious involves more than just asking questions and devouring literature. It involves being adaptable and looking beyond the obvious. Some individuals find this task challenging. They are unable to decide on a home to buy or rent because they dislike the kitchen wall colour. Or they do not wish to relocate to a different city or neighbourhood. They are native people.

They planted their roots and intend to maintain them there.

These situations may represent personal preferences or idiosyncrasies, but when they prevent us from following God's leading in our lives, that's a serious matter.

How often have you missed opportunities or adventures God called you to pursue? You lowered your head and stated, "No thanks." Today is not the day. I'm not curious in the least. I'm content where I am and with what I'm doing."

Queen Sheba was inquisitive. According to 1 Kings 10:1-13, her curiosity led her to seek out a man who trusted in the God of Israel. Was everything said about King Solomon accurate? Were the tales accurate? Her inquisitiveness and willingness to leave her native land exposed her to the source of Solomon's wisdom. After challenging him with difficult questions, she left believing she had only heard half of his greatness.

When we seek God's wisdom, he directs our questions, reveals the answers, and illuminates our minds.

"Obtaining wisdom is the most prudent course of action" (Proverbs 4:7 NLT).

Be Educatable

When was the last time you asked a question and disliked the response? You desired someone's advice, but you rejected it when it was given. That is inquisitiveness without teachability.

It is equivalent to saying, "I want your advice, but I won't follow it. I am interested in what you have to say, but I am unwilling to listen." How frequently do we do this with one another? How often do we treat God in this manner?

Listening is a form of art. Being a good listener is a skill. We hear words without truly understanding what is being said. We listen to words without observing what the body is communicating. And we hear words without reading between the lines to understand what the speaker is trying to convey. When we only hear with our ears, we are not truly listening. We cannot be instructed.

Being teachable is both an art and a skill. If we do not have a teachable heart to absorb and apply what we are being taught, we are merely absorbing information. Mind is exercised while the heart becomes dull.

You are familiar with Martha's invitation to Jesus and his disciples in Luke 10:38-42. She busied herself with the preparation of all meals. Mary, meanwhile, sat quietly and listened to Jesus. Jesus responded to Martha's complaint about Mary's lack of assistance by saying, "My dear Martha, you are anxious and upset about all these details. There is only one thing that warrants concern. Mary has found it, and no one can take it away from her."

Have you ever pondered Martha's actions following Jesus' rebuke? Martha's attitude reappears in John 11:17–44 in the account of Lazarus. Here, Martha informs Jesus of his tardiness and the fact that Lazarus has been dead for four days. She wanted to ensure that Jesus was aware of the situation's particulars. Jesus replied, "Did I not say you would see the glory of God if you believed?"

Being detail-oriented and somewhat of a perfectionist myself, I've often felt that Martha has been unfairly portrayed throughout history. She was not awful. She simply had the wrong priorities, and her focus on the details prevented her from seeing the big picture. I believe

Martha was, however, teachable. "Yes, Lord, I have always believed that you are the Messiah, the Son of God, who has come into the world from God," she replied to Jesus in John 11:27, indicating that she was a woman of great faith. Martha may have been a slow learner in certain areas, but her faith, her interactions with Jesus, and his patience with her brought her to a place where she was teachable.

Chapter 17: Developing The Right Attitude

The first step you must take to reach your full potential and achieve life's abundance is to adopt the proper mindset.

Overflow mindset is one of the most popular and recommended attitudes. This is the exact opposite of the mindset of scarcity.

Intellectual deficiency is primarily rooted in the fear of having insufficient resources and the dread of shedding possessions.

You are living under the delusion that your stockpile, assets, lovers, and companions are limited if you have this mindset. Uncertainty is unquestionably present here.

The Outlook

Nonetheless, an overflowing mindset is founded on confidence and vitality. This demonstrates that you unequivocally accept that you have unlimited resources to accomplish your daily needs. That life has no need for money-related problems. You can achieve this by recognising that money is abundant in the world. You realise that even if one opportunity doesn't pan out, there are still a multitude of other opportunities waiting for you to discover them. Never again will this have such a negative impact on you.

People who live with an overflow attitude, or who have the right mentality, do not fear difficult situations or obstacles, because regardless of whether things turn out as they want or as they plan, there are still a great deal of opportunities in front of them - opportunities that can help them achieve overflow in various aspects of their lives.

Each person possesses the novel ability to reveal everything they require without restriction. Indeed, all you wish for is to possess and equip yourself with the proper disposition and mentality. Here are some qualities you should possess to attract abundance in your daily life.

•Gratitude: No matter your situation in life, there are a multitude of things for which you should be grateful. Being appreciative and appreciating even the smallest details will attract more good fortune into your life.

- Conviction: Have faith in yourself and your capacity to create your own predetermination and reality through your actions.

contemplations. These are the keys to your internal identity and inner power. Self-doubt can be harmful; it may prevent you from achieving success and advancing in daily life.

- Make a move: The universe provides you with numerous opportunities that will lead you directly to achieving your goals. Whenever extraordinary opportunities present themselves, take action. Try not to believe that karma will perform supernatural occurrences on your behalf; instead, do your own thing and take sensible action.

- Never attempt to coerce something to occur; learn how to let go. You will be agitated and provoked if you are compelled to cause a specific event to occur. Always, there is a rationale for why things occur. However, even if it's true, you can turn things around because you have the unique ability to do so.

In fact, the best way to achieve genuine overabundance in life is by adopting the proper mentality. Life should be blissful and joyful; enjoy what you're doing and ensure that your genuine zeal is effectively communicated.

Keep in mind that the force of attracting abundance lies within yourself and the correct perspective.

Chapter 18: Spend on Yourself

You have gained a thorough understanding of the fundamentals of leadership and how to become an ideal role model for your team. Now is the time to concentrate on yourself. So far, we've discussed how you can devote all of your time and energy to serving your company and your team. Now, let's examine how you can serve yourself and your career. Especially as a woman leader, you might not have as many mentors. You must take care of yourself, watch out for yourself, and invest in yourself above all else. Your skill set is the most important aspect of your career, and honing it constantly will propel you to the pinnacle of your ambitions. This chapter will dissect how self-investment can be incorporated into your career.

Knowledge of Oneself

You must know yourself prior to getting to know your employees and their professional identities. Spend some time in your professional development learning about your strengths, weaknesses, and interests. Learn how you react during a crisis and how you handle criticism. Understanding who you are is the first step in attempting to better yourself. Your development as a leader depends on understanding your starting point. This section will examine how self-awareness can help you become a better leader.

Leadership Importance of Self-Awareness

As a leader, you should present your employees with a clear and consistent image of who you are. But how can you do this if you are not first convinced? Before projecting an image of yourself as a leader, you must first develop your own leadership identity. To accomplish this, you must combine getting to know yourself in your natural state with constructing an identity that will enable you to develop into the self-assured and empowered leader you aspire to be. Once you've accomplished this, your employees will have a clear role model from whom they can seek direction and leadership. Similar to being aware of your biases, being aware of your flaws is the first step toward overcoming them, so don't be afraid to embrace the messier aspects of your personality. Every aspect of yourself is a growth opportunity. Remember that self-awareness is the foundation of self-respect, and self-respect is necessary for any leader to be as effective as possible.

Key Aspects of Self-Consciousness

How do you achieve this level of self-awareness? What questions should you ask yourself, and what personality characteristics should you evaluate?

There are many facets to a person, both professionally and personally, so you must be willing to examine yourself from all angles in order to thoroughly examine all aspects of yourself. In order to build a solid foundation for self-awareness, this section will provide a list of key traits that you should examine honestly.

Personality Attributes

Each individual has a distinct set of personality traits. There are numerous experiences and characteristics that distinguish each individual. Consequently, you should view yourself as an individual with a distinct personality profile. You might think you know yourself, but if you haven't asked yourself the tough questions, you might not know yourself as well as you think. Try taking a personality quiz; it can be as lighthearted as the ColorCode, as straightforward as a quiz about the type of leader you are, or as intense as a Myers-Briggs personality test. Even if the results are not 100 percent accurate, you can gain a great deal of insight by considering the questions they pose. You could consider whether you are more introverted or extroverted, intuitive or perceptive, free-spirited or task-oriented. These descriptors will assist you in creating a clear image of who you are. The most important aspect of personality profiles is that they do not discuss positive or negative traits. They neutrally describe the nature of your personality, allowing you to see the various ways in which you may operate and where you fall on the quiz's results scale without necessarily passing judgement. They can also assist you in recognising how to combat some of your weaknesses while remaining consistent with your existing personality. So, for instance, suppose you are a more independent person who struggles with meeting deadlines. The solution is not to become a task-oriented individual, but to make your free-spirited personality function within the context of deadlines. This way, you will be aware of the areas in which you need to improve, rather than attempting to alter your entire personality. You are a unique individual with much to offer the world, so there is no need to fundamentally alter who you are. With the proper care and accommodations, any personality type is capable of achieving professional success.

Personal Values

In addition to your personality, you should be conscious of the values you project to the world. These can be the moral compass that guides your life, as discussed in Chapter 5, but they can also be political and spiritual beliefs. For this evaluation, consider the things that give your life meaning. Is it related?

Activism? Religion versus community Accessing the essence of your life's values is the basis for identifying your opinions and goals. Once you have identified the things that are meaningful to you, you can begin to construct a profile of your personal values. You can categorise them as interpersonal values (Kindness? Boundaries? Communication?), religious values (Faith? Humility? Commitment?), professional values (Innovation? Punctuality? Advocacy?), and many others. Working in an environment that completely contradicts your beliefs will be detrimental to your health. However, working for a company that shares your values will provide significantly more fulfilment. Living your values will benefit you personally and professionally by guiding you to perform meaningful work that is in line with your values.

Behavior

You should also be conscious of your typical behaviour. You can think of this as being externally related to your personality profile. While your personality profile may focus on your innermost feelings and most private thoughts, the behaviour section examines what you actually do and how you interact with the outside world. The good news is that you are not alone in evaluating this aspect of yourself due to its visibility to others. You can solicit the opinions of others. Obviously, self-reflection should come first, but you can supplement this with the input and observations of others to gain a fresh perspective on your habits. Ask yourself (or others) the following: "What is my typical response to a crisis?" or "Am I skilled at counselling my employees emotionally?" These questions will assist you in evaluating your actual behaviour, providing you with a deeper level of self-awareness and the ability to initiate self-improvement. Knowing that you are an introvert is one thing, but knowing that you do your best work while alone in your office listening to music is a more useful piece of information for self-improvement.

CHAPTER 19: IT IS TIME TO ASSUME LEADERSHIP

Rather than placing people into categories based on their beliefs, the world requires strong leaders with the ability to meet them where they are. Many people are currently disconnected from their internal guidance, operating out of fear and according to other people's rules. Inconsistent with their design, they are directing. This is a significant contributor to burnout and disillusionment. The ways in which people operate and their strengths are truly exquisitely diverse. Human Design's greatest gift is the ability to recognise, appreciate, and work with this.

All designs are flawless. Rather than focusing on "weaknesses," it is time to encourage leaders to embody their designs more fully, lead from a position of strength, and trust their decision-making process. My job is to assist leaders in living their designs, defining their goals, and moving toward them so that they can lead in all aspects of their lives rather than being influenced by external events and circumstances. When people operate from this position, they can achieve success even if their company culture values a different design.

As stated previously, I have spent over twenty years in corporate leadership roles and over twenty years in the spiritual development industry creating and leading communities. I am well-versed in supporting people to achieve success in life, to face their fears, to let go of self-defeating beliefs, and to lead from their strengths. This is my life's work. I am here to assist leaders in developing a strong relationship with their inner guidance and a sense of trust in it. I assist individuals in overcoming obstacles by utilising a variety of tools. Using Human Design, I am able to see their entire operating system at a glance, zero in on potential stumbling blocks quickly, and offer advice based on their wiring.

I'm writing this just a few days after returning from Jack's birth, my first grandchild. Augusts' supermoon was at its peak when he arrived in this world after a long and arduous journey. As I first held him in my arms, I was awestruck by his beauty, completeness, and perfection. All of his needs are met despite his fragile condition. This aspect of his charm is that he is wholly himself. His rational mind has not yet come online to tell him what he should be, where he needs improvement, or where he falls short of some ideal.

It was a privilege to be present for his birth. Due to the fact that I was able to record the precise time, I was able to examine his Human Design and gain a sense of his profound soul. Then I recalled the first time I held my children, when I desperately desired a parenting guide. It turns out that both of my children have a learning profile that requires them to first collect information and then learn through trial and error. People with this learning style are predisposed to figure things out on their own because they are independent. As a young mother, I felt helpless because my children rejected my advice. I believed it was my fault that what I had to say was unimportant. If I had known that this is how my children are built, I would have adjusted my parenting approach accordingly.

Chapter 20: Develop Personal Power Abilities

Since we are our own worst critics, we frequently pay more attention to our flaws than to our virtues. However, according to experts, focusing on a single area can help you achieve success more quickly than attempting to improve every aspect of your life or fix all of your flaws. Changing a single aspect of your life can provide you with a new perspective on who you are, boost your confidence and self-esteem, and prepare you for future changes. In addition, you can increase your power by focusing on changing a few of your characteristics.

We are guilty of harshly criticising ourselves for past errors and comparing ourselves to those we perceive to be vastly superior. It is one of the most delicate things we can do for ourselves to forgive and forget. Consider the positive things you have accomplished each day, and be proud. Do not worry about circumstances outside of your control.

Practicing gratitude is one of the most acceptable ways to alter your perspective of yourself and those around you. A grateful disposition makes us happier and more sociable. It also enhances our enjoyment. Your child will quickly grasp the concept of gratitude if they are surrounded by appreciative individuals, objects, and role models. Many individuals find it beneficial to compile a list of at least three things for which they are grateful each day.

You can also improve your strength by performing the provided exercises.

Chapter 21: Introduction Based on Positive Strengths

Shifting your attention to more uplifting areas of life is one method to concentrate on your strengths rather than your faults. You are given a chance to think back on, remember, and describe instances when they successfully leveraged your abilities through strength-based introductions.

In this exercise, you'll write about a period when they performed at their peak and then consider the character traits they exhibited.

The Strengths Self-Efficacy measure can evaluate your capacity to identify and leverage your distinctive strengths in various contexts, including work, family, and academic settings.

You should know your top five trademark strengths and be familiar with the pertinent strength definitions to complete this exercise. Identify their five defining qualities. Then, give each of the following judgments a score between 1 (not at all assured) and 10: (extremely confident). For example, "How self-assured are you in your capacity to use your strengths at school?" and "How self-assured are you in your capacity to use your strengths to assist you in achieving your objectives in life?" are statements that are focused on your perception assurance in their capacity to use each of their five top strengths successfully.

Chapter 22: The Evaluation of Strength

Maintaining your growth could be challenging. By evaluating your development, you have the opportunity to acknowledge your development and create a physical reminder of your hard work and dedication. This exercise aims to highlight and sustain your progress by incorporating frequent and encouraging assessments throughout the procedure.

You should create a descriptive report card outlining your strengths, assets, and growth, as well as a section assuming ongoing change. When your report card is complete, share it with your family or a close friend so you can discuss the information and formulate a plan for your next steps.

Chapter 24: Managing Your Free Time

In the preceding section of the book, you were introduced to every aspect of time management. It has been stated repeatedly that you must maximise the available time. Ultimately, time management is related to the quality of your life and the level of satisfaction you experience, and it affects every other aspect of life. However, you also require some free time. It is not enough to simply take time off from work; one must also learn how to maximize it. This provides you with a much-needed break from everyday stresses and allows you to pursue activities you enjoy.

Remember that your body and mind are not indestructible machines. It can be quite tempting to work nonstop in the mistaken belief that you are being more productive. You cannot rest and recuperate if you do not take necessary breaks between tasks. This means that you may experience the negative effects of being overworked, such as high levels of stress, a lack of concentration, and an overall feeling of being overwhelmed. A break allows you to focus on something else and utilize your time as you see fit. If you have any hobbies, interests, or passions, now is the time to pursue them. You can also use your free time to review or brush up on an old skill or to acquire any new skills that will advance your professional career.

Chapter 25: How Much Time Is Available?

The first step in maximizing your time is determining how much time you have available. Unless you know how much time you have, it is impossible to make appropriate plans. After this, you can begin to consider how it will be spent. This allows you to identify tasks that are not only realizable, but also feasible within the available time frame.

To determine your available free time, you must consider your current obligations and any impending changes. Take some time for yourself and write in a journal. Then, make a list of all your existing obligations. These commitments will include work, home, and personal responsibilities. Keep track of everything. After this, make a list of the things that will inevitably change. For instance, if you have children at home, your time at home will vary depending on their school schedule. Similarly, noting upcoming holidays is beneficial when it comes to making the most of available time.

Chapter 26: Clear Objectives Are Required

The second aspect is to ensure that your intentions regarding how you wish to spend your free time are crystal clear. You may already know or have a general idea of what you typically enjoy doing. You may enjoy playing a sport, reading, or spending time with your friends, for instance. Similarly, there will be times when you are unsure of your intentions. It makes no difference because you can always use the available time to test and explore new things. These two steps can be followed to establish crystal-clear goals and determine the desired activities. After this, you must simply priorities. You may have a list of hobbies and activities you wish to pursue. Unfortunately, whenever you have free time, you may end up doing something entirely different. You may wish to concentrate on challenging activities in order to improve yourself. Similarly, you will want to engage in enjoyable activities. Consider activities that you want to do for their own sake or to improve your mood. During whatever you are doing, make a note.

There will be various activities you will wish to prioritise. Now is the time to set priorities. After all, it is impossible to do everything at once. Instead, begin with one thing before moving on to the next. For example, having as much fun as possible during your free time may be a top priority. This implies that the majority of your free time must be spent engaging in activities you enjoy. Or you may wish to prioritise productivity and education. In this case, you will need to acquire new knowledge whenever you have the opportunity.

Chapter 27: Be a Bit Adaptable

After completing the first two steps, you likely believe that without planning, you cannot maximize the available time. However, flexibility is required when it comes to unwinding. Your leisure time does not have to be as regimented as your working hours. Instead, the focus is on adaptability. Life is always unpredictable. For instance, you may have different weekend plans than your neighbour. Unfortunately, a crucial project at work necessitates that you work longer hours. In such a situation, disappointment is normal. However, rather than dwelling on the disappointment, focus on completing the current task so that you can move on to something else. You can manage your expectations by learning to be somewhat adaptable.

Chapter 28: What Can an absence of leadership lead to

Today's leaders are subjected to intense scrutiny, with people searching for their every flaw and error. Their decisions and actions are continually evaluated, criticised, and reprimanded. In the era of social media and instantaneous sharing, leaders in the public eye face accusations that are witnessed by hundreds, thousands, or even millions of people before they have the opportunity to explain or defend themselves. Social media has drastically reduced the time between breaking news and public reaction, which has a significant impact on businesses. A few clicks are sufficient to generate a costly media issue in terms of compensation and lost revenue.

As a result, contemporary leaders must control their impact and act prudently. They require the skills and abilities necessary for effective, unifying leadership. Unfortunately, not all executives demonstrate leadership. In reality, being an effective leader requires more than providing the necessary management and oversight to achieve the team's goals. Examining the descriptions of core qualities typically associated with a leadership position makes the job considerably more complicated.

Taking this research a step further, we find that truly excellent leaders are aware of their own strengths and weaknesses. They are aware of the factors that could derail them and their behaviour under pressure. They are then taught techniques for managing the negative effects of their dark side. They recognise that if they are derailed, their behaviour may have a significant, and possibly irreparable, impact on their reputation and the performance of the company.

Chapter 29: Here are some potential consequences of ineffective leadership:

Never before have concerns about the integrity of leaders been so widespread. Leaders deserving of confidence are in greater demand than ever before as a result of scandals that have damaged world leaders in recent years. The capacity to inspire confidence is related to the ideals of accepting responsibility for one's actions and their consequences, fulfilling professional obligations, and behaving impeccably with team members. The more people observe these characteristics in leaders, the more they lend credibility and legitimacy to those leaders. And the organization's reputation improves with the degree to which executives are able to inspire confidence. Bad leaders have a much more difficult time motivating not only employees, but also business partners, colleagues, and other stakeholders, which can have a direct impact on the performance of the organisation.

Formal or informal, influence is the fundamental element of leadership. Putting someone in a leadership position does not always imply that people will follow them; they will follow them if their vision and beliefs inspire confidence. It is necessary for others to recognise and appoint leaders. Influential people use a combination of their attributes, such as charisma, and techniques to promote their ideas, convince others of the veracity of their perspectives, and encourage them to participate in their endeavours.

Ineffective leaders will not be able to persuade their employees, coworkers, or employers to achieve the desired results. They will encounter key players who are hesitant to commit to a change or invest their resources at the appropriate time. As a result of a manager's poor leadership, it is possible that their ideas will be rejected, despite the fact that they could be beneficial to the organisation.

In certain situations, leaders may be required to choose between two concepts, visions, or action plans. If only one option is available, a strong leader must be able to promote alignment and ensure that all stakeholders are satisfied with the selection.

If leaders cannot make a decision and guarantee unambiguous alignment, their reputation could be in jeopardy. Leaders who adopt the improper strategy may be perceived as inconsistent or indecisive. They could alienate those involved in the decision-making process and cause divisions within the team.

Leaders can't get very far on their own, which is why they need an effective team. They are responsible for establishing and nurturing this team in order to achieve ambitious goals. They must adopt management strategies that enable employees to utilize their skills, feel that their efforts are significant, make a positive contribution to achieving company goals, and achieve success. Leaders are responsible for providing their team members with assistance and opportunities for professional development, as well as tasks suited to their abilities. This is how they can inspire people to take responsibility for and exert effort toward their professional development.

It will be challenging for ineffective leaders to recruit and develop competent personnel. They will have difficulty identifying key players who can help them compensate for their weaknesses. And this will have an effect on the overall performance of the team.

Organizations that survive are those that implement effective collaborative work practices both within and outside the business. To establish a cooperative work environment, leaders must possess exceptional interpersonal skills that allow them to build bridges and maintain valuable network ties. This enhances the exchange of information and the resolution of problems.

Negative emotions related to ineffective leadership can extend beyond the immediate team. The actions of a poor leader can have a negative impact on the work environment and the quality of outside collaborations.

People seek meaning in their work and want to comprehend the impact of their day-to-day activities on the enterprise. Employees want to believe that their work is valued by others and that their ideas and opinions are considered. The contribution of each team member can be highlighted by a good leader, who may also inspire the group.

Bad leaders, on the other hand, have difficulty demonstrating the added value of each employee, which makes it more difficult to form genuine partnerships. This sort of behavior results in a loss of motivation, diminished performance, and the rapid departure of team members.

Who desires to place confidence in a weak leader? Follow the path laid out by a lousy leader? Or place their career in the hands of an awful leader? Poor leadership has significant repercussions, but the root cause of the issue is frequently unreported within organizations. According to a survey conducted by Hogan Assessment Systems in the United States, 78 percent of workers indicate that their immediate supervisor is the aspect of their job they dislike the most.

Thankfully, measures can be implemented to enhance professional behavior and maximize one's strengths. Making ineffective leaders aware of their influence and ensuring they understand the impact of their leadership style is the first step in the right direction. Making the transition from a poor leader to a good leader is possible... it just requires effort!

www.ingramcontent.com/pod-product-compliance
Lightning Source LLC
Chambersburg PA
CBHW050237120526
44590CB00016B/2131